Even the Cracks

poems by

Sandra Kolankiewicz

Finishing Line Press
Georgetown, Kentucky

Even the Cracks

Publisher: Leah Huete de Maines
Editor: Christen Kincaid
Cover Art: Carlo Raso via Flicker
Author Photo: Jill Ruff
Cover Design: Elizabeth Maines McCleavy

Order online: www.finishinglinepress.com
also available on amazon.com

Author inquiries and mail orders:
Finishing Line Press
PO Box 1626
Georgetown, Kentucky 40324
USA

Table of Contents

ld woman said, "Just scoop envy out
spoon, lay it on a cutting board, filleted
in pieces. Don't confuse this move
emoving jealousy, which is not the coveting
t someone else has but is instead
r he will take something of yours which he wants,
it aside to add later.
ority and entitlement will have to be carved
h a knife, but they are 'oma's' meaning 'encapsulated,'
gh deep, they pop out like whiteheads on your cheekbone,
emoved.   The higher the flame,
re the contents disappear into a broth as marrow
lo. Anxiety peels back
onion while depression's as common as baby
which for some become the main ingredient,
you, she said, you've
otten that tears are like spices,
gs like salt, that the blood you let
never burns, curdles, or evaporates
ely, and the ingredients of hope—found
de of the road—yellow like wild mustard,
unappreciated chicory, white
Queen Anne's lace that makes implantation
le if your timing's right, grow
n highway dust, bloom in all
ost impossible ground."

To the person who reads this book: thank you

Lili Fre Tells Me

When I start to think too har[d]
Lili Fre tells me stories of acci[dents]
that never happened, which [...]
according to no definition of [...]
I've ever heard. Trains
don't slide off rails like erran[t]
serpents, door latches are cli[...]
in place, pitch forks are safe
in the shed, people change
their minds at the last minu[te]
do what they should. She [wants]
me to lay aside that one
mistake and enjoy what I h[...]
Oh, Lili! I want to warn
her. You see the world so [...]
without a soul depending [...]
by past half-truths that ke[...]
you stuck in time, though[...]
is greying, your waistline
like mine, to which she a[...]
tale I've ever heard,
making me feel like the [...]
no swamp to hide in, no[...]
me so they can ask abou[t...]
tempers, what I saw or [...]
what I thought I'd be
before I became who I [...]

Old

The [...]
with [...]
into t[...]
with [...]
of wh[...]
the fe[...]
so set[...]
Super[...]
out w[...]
so tho[...]
easily[...]
the m[...]
might[...]
like an[...]
carrots[...]
but no[...]
not for[...]
yearnin[g...]
for love[...]
comple[...]
by the s[...]
blue lik[e...]
like the[...]
impossi[...]
covered[...]
but the [...]

A Box of Shells

After we assume
what we never wanted to
be, the only solution is to peel.
In seasons overly wet,
the rivers under our skin flood,
need to be dealt with,
addressed, acknowledged,
for the drought is always
coming and the ever damp
creates its own problems.
Shrinking after swelling's the
best time to shed. Be the
snake that both repulses and
makes you afraid. Find two
saplings to pin yourself between
and pull yourself through, two
branches where you can fit
to find the right pressure, or use
other objects to assist you in the scrape,
such as a person and an institution,
two friends or enemies, lovers,
whatever roles you need to slip
among and amid, rejuvenate through
giving up a layer of your outer self.
We had a box of shells we'd classify
and trade in the basement playroom,
one rainy day found a rattler skin
and rattle among the cockles,
limpets, clams, and rock oysters.

The Flames Before Us

Crouching around the fire in the dark, our bodies
steaming wet from the waterfall,
we peel oranges and toss their skins
into the blaze.
Water slips from us in droplets,
melts into the leaves and seeps
into the soft earth.

An ember collapses.
Red coals tumble beyond their stones
and live for an instant on the damp ground.

The flames before us cast our shadows
far into the forest.

Communique #11

For along with the brown lawns and the barren
       trees appearing to be old remnants
of a forest fire instead of parched from the
       long, slow drought,
                this uneasy feeling
still underpins us all because we want to
       believe we are safe, that mother and
father are there watching over us, their life
       decisions correct, outcomes foreseen,

though we don't believe imagination is
       stronger than the third dimension.
                We
cannot stop more than a tragedy
       in a day's time, for the night is so
much longer now, most of our lives being held
       in the dark, blue skies a memory,

iron the color we see now if we take
       a chance and risk disappointment.
                We
worry for children, in fact regret them.

Yucca

During the service, we perched on a bench
outside in the memory garden, a
circuitous pathway around pruned trees
and blooming rhododendrons, the caches
that would hold the urns in little clusters,
each private and with a place to sit. She
was so small her toes did not touch the ground,
lacy socks on little feet kicking in
patent leather shoes, brand new for the day
till she climbed down to watch something I could
not see on the brick walkway a few feet
ahead of us in a dapple of light,
for at that time I did not understand
I need to wear glasses always, instead
chose to accept the world as I thought it
was: indistinct and not quite graspable,
lovely but missing the equivalent
of edges. She called my name, the chorus
floating out the open door through which we'd
left when her toddler restlessness began
to irritate the surrounding ladies,
the sound of the organ floating toward us
on a breeze we could not see, and when I
joined her on the ground in my funeral
best, I saw a moth carried away in
a dignified manner by a line of
ants that were absorbed and gentle in their
own way, the kind of moth that pollinates
that old fashioned plant no one grows these days,
the name of which I could not remember.

Of Solitude and Lamplight

By dawn the cocoon of reminding
    myself of past success in order
        to survive the present dissipates in
little spirals, becoming invisible by
    transferring their energy, soon
        indistinguishable from the air and
the grass, just as I am, beginning
    with the first foot into the leg of a
        pant and ending when I finally lie
down to sleep, hours after these rays
    have given up but which now so
        alter the nature of my thoughts from
memory to prospect as I propose
    to make my way in the world, a sun
        which cannot outlast me by evening,
which will have to retire while I'll live
    into the late hours, surrounded by the
        intimacy of solitude and lamplight.

Earth at Apogee

I can't write of the seas
without seeing that landmass of
plastic swirling in the Pacific,
bigger than Pitcairn Island, the
consequences of mutiny against the
natural world. Squeeze a rock,
drain the dirt to get plastic.
Scrape a sticky flower center for the
smell of forget what we deserve.
Likewise that sacred cliff
from which the ancestors watched
us from above had no means to
protect itself, face blown off to
reveal the images of idols, their feet
down in the clay on which we stand
to admire them. We have even stripped
the sun light of vitamin d, separated the
air from the kind of fuel that fills your
bones, makes them strong enough to
climb a defiled mountain, holy hills like
those bumps in the grass that used to be
tombs before the bombing made the
skeletons of the ancient dead indistinguishable
from the recently departed. What
angry cloud set fire to the brush? Where
did the birds and bears retreat when
the forest turned to ash, earth at apogee
from itself and pulled toward perigee,
torn between who we were and who
we can become, creators of a new
continent in our own image.

In the Absence

What should I have said at work this
    morning while all flexed and jostled in
        anticipation, remembering

service and sacrifice, making
    imaginary comparisons, measuring the
        level to which each is owed,

especially those who buried
    the evidence, passed the
        authorities on to the next

department, foot on the rug
    concealing the hole in the
        floor, its covert contents

smuggled in for the few at
    personal risk. This evening,
        I leave cans of food on the porch

for the Mail Carrier Hunger
    Drive, the couple next door
        at it again, fulfilling all the

predictions except for the baby.
    Each day I rejoice in the
        absence of little eyes and ears,

the lack of pitter patter
    running away in fear. I give
        thanks I'm not the weak end of

the teeter totter, high and
    dry, too light to matter,
        unable to come down.

This Card That Says Get Well

I'd meet you on the edge except where we
used to stand has crumbled, collapsed like a
dune into the sea, calved like a glacier
meeting the water, separated like
sheering off the tip of a complacent
continent. Go get the girls, bring back the
boys, enlist the elderly, enlighten
the unemployed, chum up the choir, for the
afterlife's right here, ringing like a bell
in that space where something used to be, found
in absence and loss, passive and active
resistance. My factory became a
bedroom, my sleeping space a kitchen where
all are invited to eat, but no one
arrives. The lawn transformed to moat, driveway
drawn up like a bridge. Let me see the mask
under the face covering you're wearing,
the clothes under your nakedness, the shoes
like soles to your bare feet. You've nowhere to
go but the store, nothing to share except
stories of when we wove tales, went places,
the world an oyster left on the counter
to rot. We forgot the mollusk was there,
unopened, until the smell reminded
us of tasks and obligations. We take
out the trash, police the perimeter,
pick up paper, recycle the bags, text
a friend, send a note through the mail to a
person who might be dead, who can't recall
his name nor yours nor the whereabouts of
the one who wrote this card that says Get Well.

As Herself Even Though

The first light came like an infant who hasn't
slept the night, the sky red and screaming from her
toothless, cherry mouth. Arrange her over your
shoulder, away from your ear, and she wails at
the past, the wave you leave behind in your wake
as you walk the floor, upsetting the air and
making a path for silent molecules to
follow. Raised above you, her gaze outward
and away, she cries like a maiden bound to
the prow of a ship, bent on a voyage toward
a future she resists. Children are poor
metaphors for experience, the nurse told
me after the operation which was meant
to fix what happened in a country where they
sterilized me for free. Man, woman, rich, poor
rendered inert except for the energy
in their own lives, no taking on the privilege
of another, having survived the kind of
love that lets you see a baby as herself
even though she's yours and wailing at the dawn.

Stars in the Mouth

If you had done nothing, you would have made
　　no mistakes, what you try to remember
　　　　when you're down in the hole, looking around
　　　　　　for someone else to save, metaphor,
of course, for you haven't adventured since
　　you decided you failed the tree you
　　　　were trying to help, or the wrong person
　　　　　　got elected. In spite of your efforts.
I know too much about you to ignore
　　your multiple sources of water, the
　　　　stream, the river, the lake, all the places
　　　　　　you tried to wash yourself clean as if some
one would hold you under, stand on fingers
　　at the edge of a dock to punish you
　　　　for dropping something on land. No place smells
　　　　　　like a hemlock grove, but you don't live there,
can merely visit, occupy in thought
　　or imagination, turning the pin
　　　　pricks of lights on the other side of the
　　　　　　lake into stars in the mouth of your well.

Last Night We Lit a Bonfire
For Hunt Brawley

I cannot stop considering the geese
honking to one another across the
icy pond, the snapper estivating
below the mud in a darkness blacker
than sleep, soon to come around according
to some inner or outer signal that
lets him know the axis of the world has
tipped enough to bring him back to life. Last
night we lit a bonfire, ridding ourselves
of the kind of scraps you can burn when
you've renovated an old bathroom: left
over blocks of pine studs, enough to get
the damp limb of the Norway maple lit
so we could feed it to the flames all night
long with the smaller branches and fat twigs
that gave up in the wind storm which took two
of our slates last week. This might be the last
coat I ever buy, you mused, sitting with
your boots propped on the rocks of our fire ring,
thinking of your father's brown tweed hunting
jacket hanging in our closet, the one
you sometimes wear and which outlasted him.

The Art Table

For by then I had given up speaking
at all, not quick enough to gather my
thoughts together and package them into
any utterance that could compete with
the voices of those who surrounded me. My
throat hurt from swallowing all I wanted
to say, my cheeks flushed while I formed ideas,
but the rest of the world moved on. We had
two kinds of windows, those I could see out
of and ones with sills taller than I could
stand. In some rooms I was a prisoner,
in others an observer, at times a
participant who clung to the wall like
a fly, watched at the same time she performed.
The first day at the art table, I drew
a ship that would take me away, then a
cart with a buggy that would clip clop clip
clop me down the road, and a bicycle
with streamers flying in wind I pedaled.

As the Coffee Brews
For Cheryl Cesta

You roll from bed before dawn, press the button
on the coffee maker, stand on the front
porch, your mother's old mumu
thrown on like a tent of respectability. The bats
are back to resting in neglected chimneys
or in the eaves of old carriage houses become tilting
garages among one hundred twenty
year old housing stock taken for granted, rented
to destruction and barely maintained, dented, some
windowless, all the floors in the neighborhood red
pine bought off a railroad car from the
South, a wood which doesn't exist anymore,
the frames cut from unimaginable oaks,
the size you see now only on private lands
and in nature parks. The birds have started
though darkness is still full, their chirps
letting the rest of the world know
the moment to put away the night
with its musky comfort and deep secrets
has arrived, time to wear your mother's
impossible colors as the coffee brews.

Would Recognize

I'm not sure what to say of the grim-faced men
pushing people up the steps of the trains we
were so thrilled to see updated, modernized
cars floating on magnetic tracks at a speed
unimaginable to my grandmother
who never would have believed you could ride the
Staten Island ferry with a phone in your
pocket. My earliest memory's of pointing
to the great lady with the torch, appearing
both gigantic and small under a grey sky,
withstanding the raindrops that fell as we moved
below to sit in our scratchy, woolen coats.
A year in Chicago after her hasty
marriage, from the window of their new high rise,
they watched a tornado plow the city on
the other side of town and wanted to go
home. Who can blame them for knowing a lake was
not the sea, for craving neighborhood grit, for
missing their mothers and aunties, thinking a
bay their home, an island their oasis? She
never left again, knitted socks for soldiers
in two wars, could admit drawing a line and
holding was the same as losing, claimed painful
events are sometimes meant to be forgotten,
would recognize what is happening today.

Ritual

I couldn't wait to become a sook
    after my pubertal molt, thrilled when
my urine began to produce that
    pheromone which would bring you to me.
You vied for me on the sandy floor,
    standing up high on the tips of your
walking legs, fully extending your
    reach toward me, stretching yourself out wide
so I could smell you, even causing
    another suitor to lose both his
swimming paddles. How you danced to win
    me till I turned around backward and
wedged myself under you, even let
    you subdue my flailing by tapping
and rubbing my claws with yours while I
    quieted. Then we became a buck
and rider. Soon you cradle-carried
    me off until my next molting would
occur, our courting a matter of
    seven days in which you never let
me go and I lost my shell, soft
    enough to mate, *gonopod* meeting
gonospore with injection piston
    assist!--the last time I shed. After,
you clasped and carried me again for
    two days, our postcopulatory
embrace, right side up, facing away
    from you again till my shell fully
hardened. Then you released me to swim
    with others across the open bay
to seek the higher salinity
    we would need to successfully spawn

LiLi Fre on Tears

She doesn't care the man she turned down for
being so self-absorbed is now famous.
What she remembers is he brought himself
to tears, thinking if he cried, she'd give in.
He chased her hair and ass and the little
scar above her upper lip from a dog
bite. Because she resisted, he wanted
to win. He even came to spend the night
after she married, said he was passing
through, needed somewhere to stay, just to see
for himself what she'd become, do the kind
of judging he always did everywhere
he went. *He'd fall in love*, she says, *just to
get a script from it.* Alone and glad, she has
some friends, is what you might call
'old,' though others would name her 'young.' *I think
I've failed at as much as I've succeeded*, she
says. *Sometimes when they cried, I believed them.*

The Wind Outside Raging

You were to come for dinner at seven
where I was house sitting for a couple
gone to Maine. Instead, you arrived after
midnight. The candles had melted down to
the base of the ceramic holder and
sputtered out, the meal cold, but I let you
in. Upstairs, I thought you'd know more about
women, but you took care of yourself, then
fell asleep. I rose and did the dishes,
never went back to the pillow where you
awoke at dawn to catch a two-day train
to go out West, lost until the next time,
when I was living in a cabin in
the woods. After a winter storm, I took
you to the caves, our feet squeaking in the
hush until you grabbed a stick to thump the
tree trunks we were passing, making the snow
drop off in sheets, drowning out the scolding
blue jay, the invisible wood pecker
knocking away up high, the crow cawing
as he sounded the alert, unneeded
because the whole world knew by then you were
in the forest and did not understand
enough to be quiet in the presence
of majesty. You had a beard and told
strangers your name was Abraham, said your
mother wrote letters you never finished.
I did not shave, told strangers loving them
meant nothing, both of us with our simple
lies, my stilled tears while you slept in tangled
covers, foreign to each other even
with a fire and the wind outside raging.

Stealing Me Away

I left the house before I knew where to
go, whether I should slip below the creek's
surface and cling to the cloudy
clumps of frog eggs gathered like a
million tiny eyes around the
stones at the bottom, or find a
place to rest where the deer make
nests in brambles by the edge of the
field. I sought the old cluster of tall white
pine, stared down at the red needled
floor, listening for what to do.
I stood in the frost, gazed at the barn
for belonging. By then I'd forgotten
how to push the hair from my eyes,
did not recognize myself whether coming
or going, saw my hand either making
up beds or turning their covers down.
What is the meaning of deep pools
among rocks, I wondered, if once I've
embraced the polliwogs in the stream
I become the bass below that eats them,
confused by where I end and something else
begins, neither fish nor amphibian, mere
human, afraid both of what lives at the
bottom of still water and becoming it.
I'm not yet the clothes in the closet back
there, I reminded, nor am I all the words
I cannot say, my voice soothed by
silence, these paths stealing me away.

Day of the Dead

We know by now you could still call, tap that
low landline voltage to let us know we
can let go of you, lay you in that basket
of rushes that floats away in our minds,
finds you living with a pharaoh until
you return to lead us through the desert
and receive your dry commandments, what all
patriarchs do. Surely where you are you
see a way to let us know you arrived
and are there yet beyond the veil, bumping
in the night, coins dropping from another
world and ringing off the table, the lights
flickering on without switch, dark thumps, a
deep sigh that fills the house first with the sound and
then the absence of exhalation, as
I search for you under the stairs when they
are creaking, after I've splintered into
parts that act independently yet make
up the whole, each of them looking, looking
for you, seeking still. What are the rules of
disengagement and separation in
the next dimension, when a dot becomes
a line which transforms to a box with length,
depth, and height, then steps beyond the space we
think we understand, mistaking little
toe for the entirety of body,
like misreading a beginning for an
end, confusing this current world with life.

In Wintering Holes Deep Below

If because of your weak ankles, replaced
hip or knee, or slight dizziness that makes
you stagger and bump into the door frame
as you pass through, if you cannot make your
way down to the river, either climbing
its rugged banks, walking along the bike
path, or by sitting on one of those new
benches suspended like swings at water's
edge, if when the temperature drops, your
bones ache like they're thick with frost, and for days
in a row you simply cannot get your
body warm enough to leave the house and
wander among others in their masks toward
the overlook, I want you to know the
blue heron that stands daily where the stream
meets the river under the interstate
bridge took off when he saw me today and
headed toward the refuge. A clicking king
fisher swooped away, lit on a branch, and then
swooped further off again! In spite of the
thin layer of ice in the shallow pools
along the shore, a blue jay still scolded
me. The red hawk circling high above the
grey water cried to a mate I could not
see, catfish silent, clustered together
till spring in wintering holes deep below.

As Important as the Wind

Again, the end of one life and the
    beginning of another. My mother
dies on someone else's birthday, this
    devastating event someone's best night
ever. My shoulders ache, the
    wordless grief demanding at the same time
unknown hearts elsewhere swell with success
    and gratitude. Negative, positive,
and—for one who needs mass to know where
    his body is in space--ground, attachment
necessary as a root, sailboat
    useless without a keel, and you're that drag
which makes movement forward possible,
    for me, balancing below the surface
with what's been built above on a craft most
    clearly designed by someone else, yet
my sole inheritance. Devils sprawl
    around tables below deck, do shots of
whiskey whether they're happy, bereaved,
    or clinging somewhere in the middle, the
funereal found in the constant
    drive to drown nerves overwrought from coming
face to face for eternity with
    the human weakness of the day. We work
side by side together at the pumps
    like shanghaied sailors, the ocean breaking
in us with a boned anatomy
    on which too much depends, resisting the
blood's urge to run itself aground, our
    potential hydrogen identical
to the sea, the diurnal tides lost
    to those who ignore the barometric
signs and to others who fail to see
    they're nearing the equator, float marooned
in the doldrums with no provisions,
    poor notions of what it means to have a
sail, keel as important as the wind.

Even the Cracks

For Frank Norton

I don't miss his wit, nor his slightly chipped
front tooth, his 1965 Volvo 122,
which he called his Vulva, nor his 1969
Triumph Bonneville. I'll be fine without the
upturned horse shoe over his front door,
salt water fish tank's glow-in-the-dark coral,
the Venus in a Half Shell mosaic floor he
started in his front hall, then gave up
on after setting the face, the blue eyes
and pouting lips he avoided stepping
on out of respect and made me do the same.
He moved me into and out of two
marriages, once in the middle of the
night, and liked me not as some extension of
himself, but wanted to see me grow into
who I might become in spite of those
mistakes he called moments of
enlightenment, going backwards not an option,
moving forward impossible,
scooting sideways better that staying where
I was, what he called my crab consciousness
merely his description for my either avoiding or digging
a hole, coming out when all was safe
like a ghost would. I hear him even louder
than this ringing in my ears, a sound he labeled
an attempt by enlightened beings
to communicate with me truths I do
not want to hear, spirits invisible to me in
the shower but who know my every
move and forgive me when I stray,
who don't judge me because the kind of
judging we do in three dimensions is impossible
without a body, and this is all the body I'll
ever get, he said, so make sure I
visit every inch, even the cracks.

Sabino Canyon

For Bruce Malesk

At dawn the bus dropped us at the top
of the canyon to follow the river
trail to the bottom, our lone companion
a saguaro dominating the stripped
horizon, for we knew where we stood had
once been sea, the parched cliffs in the distance
a submerged waterline with fish darting in
and out among cracks. One world can replace
another, and ours was shifting, migrants
dying fifty miles south in the valley,
trying to follow a stream which vanished,
hid itself underground in an attempt
to survive, seeking that first ocean. The
human body leaves minerals behind,
perhaps a stain on the ground underneath,
but for those seeking water all bones dry
quickly before they scatter. There, we talked
in whispers as we descended, except
when the river roared between boulders to
silence us, the only visitors to
begin the journey so early, and to
take so much time coming down, the last ones
to return so the rangers could go home.

Or Some Other, More Invisible

You are nursing a wound while wanting to
pick it, a duality of purpose,
the drive both to heal and self-destruct that
pushes people to stay still, for silence
is the only way you'll hear the cry of
the cat trapped in a closet, the noise of
your own thoughts as the electric pulses
they are, regain the subtlety of sound
you lost in the din when you were moving
out in the world.

              We yet come together
and feast, still put forgiveness on a dish
for all to eat, by now leaving off the
bowls of shame and other unhealthy plates,
ones that keep circulatory systems
so inflamed the walls of our arteries
are like sand paper snagging platelets as
they slide by.

             Is this the wound, I wonder,
this universal swelling, the loss of
ebb and flow between cells become a sort
of homeostasis, the sitting and
minding your bifurcated urges, or

some other, more invisible, dent in
the spirit that allows me to see your
arriving and leaving all at once, or

do you have an injury I can touch,
as if you burned your wrist on the oven
rack while baking someone you love a pie.

To Seek Gladness Alone

You were changed after the first time, never
        the same, whatever you want to call the
culling that occurred after you left. I
        understand what falling in love with the
forbidden means, how melancholy can
        supply us with excuses to behave
badly when, except for a few golden
        memories, we're not meant to be content.
Instead we're thoughtful, which often leads to
        joy, but not for long, considering the
state of the world. "To seek gladness alone
        is an insult to those who suffer," I
recently said to my mother, to whom
        I have begun to address my pressing
concerns as if she were still living

Parrot

I don't know what to say as I listen,
for the hearing is more important than
my desire to chime in, advise, talking
bird, tilting my head to look at you, the
world beyond my perch, clipped wings, sole chain on
my thin leg. I could say the lawn needs trimmed
or the girl next door is moving out to
shack up with her lover, who's not you, though
you still wish it. A full beer sweats on the
counter. I'll live one hundred years and, when
you die, have no forest to return to.

Reverse Zoonosis

By that time, I had driven to the desert
beyond the reach of towers and land lines,
in a camper tucked under a rock
shelter, shaded from the sun
and the heat of day by afternoon.
At dawn while I sat by the smoldering
ring of the night's fire,
I saw bats had come to roost
for the day at the other end
of the overhang, clinging together in a cluster
on the stone ceiling, lightly squeaking
and vibrating during their sleeping like a hibernating
cauldron, far enough away so we would not disturb
one another. I had parked in their home
as if I were supposed to be there to listen
to the prairie dogs and coyote, the call of the
owl, perhaps to get a dreaded
virus from them and bring back to my world,
or they'd pick up some disease from me,
pass it through the mysterious night air,
through sky as ablaze as a city
on fire, into the flicker holes in the saguaro,
thrasher nests in the Joshua trees,
into the burrows dug out by kangaroo
rats, the ground hollows of the
jackrabbits, the dens of the wolves.

The Kindness Exchange

I spent my love at the kindness exchange.
        That's what we do: invest for return. Yet
what is required from the birds that thrill me?
        And what do I give them? Is there any
other reason for the sole oak, mid field,
        besides the cattle clustered under its
cool shade at mid-day? I have no credit
        left so must invest, having overdrawn
myself while on the vacation that made me
        forget how much I reaped while neglecting
to sow, the same way we should care for roads
        or bridges, the infrastructure of our
isolated lives which takes us safely
        through the canyon, provides a guard rail when
the view is too enticing, or brings us
        water through the underground we avoid
but need to learn we depend on.

Communique #13

For we refused to
relinquish what we
had always occupied,
the space between
transition and success
no one knew was
there except those who
had fallen in, some
kind of intolerant
station where
the names were always
changing with all that
dropping down and out.
And why should we
have given up what was
always ours, walking
away from our
metaphorical date
trees and green houses,
leave them to those just
behind us? Only the
oldest counseled
that we give our
cubicles in the best
condition. One day,
they said, you will share
the fruit that comes
from that tree, and this
man you resent will
love your daughter as if
she were his own.
You'll walk the
property line together
and maintain your
fences, confine just the
cattle in your vision.

Where Life Can Grow

At first I was among those who wanted
to give up. I relinquished my effort,
just the act of turning my face away
so my gaze bent in a different arc.
Such is the work of the eye, unable
to see what pupil does not capture, the
ears not aiding unless there is sound, no
fooling with odor, for in some ways smell
is the strongest of all, can take you back
in time instantly, reduce even the
banker to a child who has lost someone
at the beach. Thus the hemlock whiff of the
place we visited each year when all were
alive, words only a means to explain
memory, not what was recalled, speech still
dependent in the end on someone to
endeavor, even when spontaneous.
Forget touch. Or don't. I have refused to
classify it, for first I would need to
divide and lack a principle that would
make all my categories complete and
distinct. Cuddles becoming sex. Patting
urged to strike. Slap to cup. Here the senses
combine like off-stage actors commenting
on the action, disagreeing so much
as to distract from the plot, making the
audience lose interest. Then the field
alters, everything tall and the windows
without glass, the horizon so flat we
can see the curve of the earth, which brings out
in some of us the urge to build a wall
to protect ourselves, provide perspective,
all straight lines needing to be broken to
inaugurate a cleft where life can grow.

ACKNOWLEDGMENTS

"Lili Fre Tells Me," *Harbinger Asylum,* October 2021
"Old Time Recipe," *Fortnightly Review,* August 2021
"A Box of Shells," *New World Writing,* May 2022
"The Flames Before Us," *Flare,* February 23, 2021
"Communique #11," *No Tokens,* March 29, 2022
"Yucca," *Typehouse,* August 8, 2020
"Of Solitude and Lamplight," *Fortnightly Review,* August 4, 2021
"Earth at Apogee," *Fortnightly Review,* August 4, 2020
"In the Absence," *Great Lakes Review,* December 31, 2021
"This Card That Says Get Well," *Drunk Monkeys,* October 2, 2021
"As Herself Even Though," *Global Youth,* March 25, 2022
"Stars in the Mouth," *Blue Mountain Review,* June 6, 2019
"Last Night We Lit a Bonfire," *8 Poems,* July 22, 2019
"The Art Table," *Kansas City Voices,* May 24, 2021
"As the Coffee Brews," *Harbinger Asylum,* October 24, 2021
"Would Recognize," *Global Youth,* March 25, 2022
"Lili Fre on Tears," *New World Writing,* May 2022
"The Wind Outside Raging," *New World Writing,* December 2021
"Stealing Me Away," *Kansas City Voices,* June 4 2022
"Day of the Dead," *New World Writing,* December 2021
"As Important As Wind," *Quibble,* June 28, 2022
"Even the Cracks," *America Magazine,* August 2022
"Sabino Canyon," *Blue Mountain Review,* October 8, 2021
"Or Some Other, More Invisible," *Beatific,* April 4, 2021
"To Seek Gladness Alone," *Healing Muse,* May 2021
"Parrot," *SoFloPoJo,* March 10, 2022
"The Kindness Exchange," *Fortnightly Review,* Aug 4, 2021
"Communique #13," *Galway Review,* June 2021
"Where Life Can Grow," *Hope Anthology,* India, July 12, 2022

Sandra Kolankiewicz's poetry and fiction have appeared widely, most recently in *Fortnightly Review, Pudding House, Heartwood,* and *Mobius.* She is the author of *Turning Inside Out, The Way You Will Go, Lost in Transition,* and *When I Fell,* a novel with 78 color illustrations by Kathy Skerritt. For her, writing poetry is a joyful phenomenon available to anyone who wishes to experience the pure delight that comes from disappearing into a creative process. Whether one is painting, drawing, singing, crafting, sculpting, dancing, or writing—whatever the activity is that takes us out of ourselves and makes time disappear while we're participating—we can all share in the positive energy that is always there for us, just waiting to be turned from wave to particle. She recently retired after four decades of teaching and lives in Marietta, Ohio.

Milton Keynes UK
Ingram Content Group UK Ltd.
UKHW010737241123
433194UK00005B/453